GOING ON SOMEWHERE

GOING ON SOMEWHERE

Poems by Karin Gustafson

Illustrations by Diana Barco
Cover by Jason Martin
Graphic design by Diana Barco and Sigma Andrea Torres

BackStroke Books

Also by Karin Gustafson
    1 Mississippi
    ManicDDaily at http://ManicDDaily.wordpress.com

GOING ON SOMEWHERE

Text copyright © 2010 by Karin Gustafson

Illustration copyright © by Diana Barco

Cover copyright © Jason Martin

Graphic design by Diana Barco and Sigma Andrea Torres

All rights reserved.

Published by BackStroke Books.

ISBN – 13: 978-0-981-99232-7

ISBN – 10: 0981992323

To Meredith, Christina, and Jay

CONTENTS

Good News/Bad News	1
Spy Games	2
Swimming in Summer	3
Have I learned anything?	4
In the dark	6
Behind the Locust	7
Beneath it all	8
Ophelia, Ophelia Syndrome	9
At Sea	10
Estranged	11
Divorce	12
Block	13
Flag	16
Veteran's Day, 2009	17
Summer Night	18
Blackberrying	19
Firefly	20
Porch	21
Pink	22

Wondrous	24
Dressed	25
Going in to look at my daughter asleep	26
No chance	27
Home	28
The Last Thing	30
What Funerals Are For	31
Burned Soldier (A Mask For Face)	32
Shattering	33
In the Ukraine, Sixty-some Years Later, Still Finding	34
Honor Killing	36
Heard on the Esplanade, a Pantoum	37
Courbet	38
Kali	39
Thin Birthday	40
Daughter Needing to Practice the Tango	41
In the Stairwell	42
A Woman Needing to Pee	43
Mismatched Couple	44
Travelers' Wedding – Bangkok	45
Cowspotting	47

For No Good Reason	48
Second Marriage	49
Lovers	50
Mist	51
Yoga Haiku	52
Truest Love	53
Side	54
After the Fights	55
Facts	56
9/11	57
Snippets	58
Post-Eden	59
No Nest	60
No Matter	61
Villanelle to Wandering Brain	62
Colaba Night (Mumbai)	63
After it's fallen	64
East Indian Trains in the Catskills	66
Jaipur	67

Good News/Bad News

And then there was the children's book
about the man, look!—who fell out of
a plane. That was the bad news.
But, phew!—he fell onto a haystack;
this was, apparently, the good news:
that his back was not broken
through the intervention of
dried grass. But, hey!—there was
a needle in that stack—bad news. Except, wait!—
he turned out to have a camel
in his pocket which fit exactly through the eye
of that needle—good news!—
for that took him straight to, do-not-pass-go to,
the kingdom of heaven, not
so much because he was a rich man
but because the haystack hadn't worked that well after all,
not against a fall from the sky.

Spy Games

We played spy games galore in the basement.
Running spy games with the boys, our bent hands
guns, till sweating we lay down on cold cement,
shirts pulled up, chests hard. Not much withstands
the leaching chill of earth, the buried sands
beneath a downstairs' room, except perhaps
the burn of nipple, the future woman's
breasts. Our spy games just for girls had traps—
some of us played femmes fatales, poor saps,
while the leader girl was Bond—0-0-7.
She hung us ropeless from the bathroom taps,
then tortured us in ways that felt like heaven,
the basement bed our rack, what spies we were,
confessing neither to ourselves nor her.

Swimming in Summer

Our palms grew pale as paws in northern climes
as water soaked right through our outer skin.
In summers past, how brightly water shines,

its surface sparked by countless solar mimes,
an aurora only fragmented by limb.
Our palms grew pale as paws in northern climes

as we played hide and seek with sunken dimes,
diving beneath the waves of echoed din;
in summers past, how brightly water shines.

My mother sat at poolside with the *Times'*
Sunday magazine; I swam by her shin,
my palms as pale as paws in northern climes,

sculpting her ivory leg, the only signs
of life the hair strands barely there, so prim
in summers past. How brightly water shines

in that lost pool; and all that filled our minds
frozen now, the glimmer petrified within
palms, grown pale as paws in northern climes.
In summers past, how brightly water shines.

Have I learned anything?

Ah this is better.
This is sitting down.
This is getting some tea.
This is biting into an orange peel, just slightly, before peeling.
This is biting into the orange.
I think about the labor leader I knew in Ahmadabad,
how they would bring him coffee
in the morning, me my tea.
He had given up tea, he told me,
when Gandhi said to, and ever since,
taking a hot slurp,
he had never drunk it.
Because of the British.

In the same way, in the car,
he took out all his toiletries, one by one, handing
them to me for examination:
a hotel soap still wrapped in its green labeled paper,
his razor, comb—he combed
his close-cropped hair before handing it to me, as if
to show its use—a small towel—
he really didn't have very much—a small
scissors. His feet up on the seat,
now he brought one to his knee, shifting
his white cloth dhoti, and
clipped the toe nails quickly, first
one foot, then the other.

He collected as he clipped
the small white crusts of nail, then
opened the window a bit wider
to toss them out.

"You see how I am always busy," he said. "Never
a moment idle, wasted. I am busy all the time,
you see how I am doing it."

I finish my breakfast slowly,
just sitting.

In the dark

I reach over in the dark to check
your cock for dreams. You push my hand away,
caught in a place well beyond my beck
and call, far distant from both the day
and the day to day. Feeling you erect,
I press into your side. But you're enthralled
inside, and feel me as a defect
in the cliff you scale as it morphs into walled
city. I touch again, press into your arms,
but you turn, intent upon some chase,
the stuff of dreams outshining my wakeful charms.
I'm jealous, yes. My brain won't make the space
for dreams these days. Ensnared in the mundane,
I wait watchfully for yours to wane.

Behind the Locust

She tiptoed under the locust trees;
their shade bared earth, her shorts bared knees.
Their bark was rough, as rough as you please,
though the wood is soft in locust trees.

Though the wood is soft, the thorns are not;
sticks fall down, and leaves on top.
She tiptoed through the thorny plot
of earth and stem and leaf and rot.

The trunk was thin but she was small
and stood at angles—so, and so—
shifting from tip to the other toe,
to hide from all who'd come and go.

No one was looking, but still she hid,
looking herself at all they did.
She watched them walking, watched them sit,
keeping close the tree's close fit.

What mystery to be lost and found
beneath the slightly rustling sound
of leaves like grapes; inside, the pound
of a heart that's longing to be grown.

Beneath it all

Beneath the red over blue sky,
she walks a darkly pitted beam;
immediately below it, gravel.
Still she holds arms out
as if balancing on a high and narrow ledge
in a harsh wind,
pretending. Pretending too
that she is a little girl; but also
pretending to be older. Younger
and older both feels cute,
like wearing, with conscious insouciance,
a too-short skirt over legs
that have learned allure.
Sure of the man watching, she
slips, then catches herself,
smiling in mock
relief, the feel of control surging through her
like growth itself.
She has much to learn.

Ophelia, Ophelia Syndrome

Girl's beast heart, age ten, swims sky,
arms swinging wings, she springs
till body turns spy—
Where does complete go?
Drips from woman's breast, ass, thigh.
She loves pining, the yearn,
craves the kiss, lick, fuck,
finds contempt, klutz lust, mucks
about in briny shyness.
Making boy-man God-king
slits wings. Rubs a zipper
into her skin to mend it,
hoards opalescence.

At Sea

The boy hauled the roses like burlap sacking—
at a distance—navigating the kitchen door,
which he kicked for noise value,
hating his mother.
What he wanted was to man
the road, casting his day by the side
of the long green wood where he
could lurk and spy and brick up
hideouts with clods of dirt and brush, never leaning
to any will except
of sky and guttering stream
to whose clear blues he'd tack
his whole young life.

Estranged

Time unrolled between them, an expansive spread.
When he thought about his brother, he thought
of sky, that huge deep blue that fed
the world out West, that blue too big to be caught
by a pair of eyes. When he thought about
his brother he thought of water, that brook
kind of water that gushed as cold as shout.
When he thought about his brother, it was like a book
come to life of all that was good, all wild,
while his own life seemed grey, sidewalk-stained,
his mind grimed by coin, his forehead defiled,
his life's rhythm the drone of the train-trained,
and he hated everything, his brother most of all,
dreaming of a time in which there'd be no grace, all fall.

Divorce

Starvation for love sands heart to sliver,
my daughter's cheeks smell of her hours with the sitter,
too sweet.
Let me have a sip—

Block

They were right-angled in the newer areas,
but our curb sloped into
a pebbled tar that bubbled below our skate wheels.
Bare knees as gravelly, the memory of
scrapes embedded in skin, we sat with them up
till the white truck jingling fairy dust
turned in, then ran for quarters.

I had a working mom and so
had funds enough for a drumstick, real
ice cream, but hid the extra change deep in a pocket
where only straight fingers could
touch bottom, joining
Patty and Susie and Celeste, the
Catholic kids, with houses of siblings,
chores, and, hovering in their stories, nuns
(rulers at the ready)—
Patty the pretty, Susie the plain,
Celeste Celeste Celeste, who, arms outstretched,
could walk across practically anything,
Celeste with the six brothers
who constantly rat-tat-tat-
played war—panting for the

popsicle of the day. Sometimes it would
be root beer, that sweet-strange amber we hardly
dared lick; pink lemonade a purer thrill
in our specific honor.
The new houses started at the next
corner but no one sat in front of their
flatter, spindly-treed, lawns.
Did those houses even
have kids?

Later, our side changed too.
Patty only came out to dry
her nails; Susie didn't feel
like playing; and Celeste, Celeste,
Celeste's father came back from
Vietnam, a different man.
Her brothers, who'd crawled under bush,
up tree, their finger guns poised,
were not to be seen.
It was dark behind
their screens, words heard only as
vibration, things shaken.

The street still,
except on the rare
blue evening as fall fell,
when a boy we'd fought
in war, lorded over on skates,
stepped out from the curb, tossing
a football hand to hand. Slowly we'd
all appear, copping moves scribbled

on his cupped palm. Our feet
slapped hard against the
pavement, voices loud that, yes, we *had*
touched with two hands.
We played until car lights glared and our
bodies smelled of cold blown leaves.
But that would be it.
We would not come out again
for some time.

Flag

There were rules. You weren't allowed to let it
touch the ground. If it did, it should be burned
or buried. You couldn't just forget it,

pretend it hadn't slipped (if stained, to wet it)—
our trusted God would see and you'd be spurned.
There were rules. You weren't allowed to let it

rip or fray. To be flown at night upset its
regimen, as it were. The darkness turned
it into something buried. Don't forget it,

leave out in the rain; you had to get it
(getting soaked yourself, your last concern).
There were rules. You weren't allowed to let it

pass—even at the movies, we would fête it—
until the Sixties came, and their war churned
and buried much—you couldn't just forget it,

pretend we hadn't slipped. The fall begat at
least two flags—one paraded, the other mourned—
but just one rule—you weren't allowed to let it
be buried; you couldn't just forget it.

Veteran's Day, 2009

My father has always worn
black, army-issue shoes,
whose toes turn up after
a few days' wear,
something from the war.

Today makes me think
of toes turned up, softly,
beneath green fields,
or stock stiff
in a sprawl of camo.

My nephew talks of joining.
I don't know what to say—
sure, if you don't get hurt,
and no one around you either,
not even those at whom you aim
your gun.

People do it, maybe have to,
even my gentle father, seventeen and
already balding, who shaved from a cup
at six a.m., then marched
twenty miles to breakfast; at Pilsen,
was issued a beer with a raw egg in it.
The man next to him
got hit, right
next to him. *And the egg,* he said,
they just drank down.

Summer Night

Frogs mince the night with
keening chants that haggle with the moon
for precedence: whether still, dead, light can outweigh
the cry of living tissue, deboning the memory
of barefoot afternoon in the black green lurk,
a leather of heavy leaf and humid longing.

Blackberrying

In a daze of phosphorescent moss,
we make our way across rock bed, log and stalk,
to a field that's sharply girded against loss
where nettle, thorn, and briar edge our walk.
Our eyes bore in on any sign of sheen,
a glisten beneath a leaf, a garnet chain.
They're hard to see at first, then like a dream
we find them here and there and there again.
First scrapes sting, branches fiercely snag skin
of wrist, arm, shin, dogged to defend their own.
We reach around, above, even step within
thickets transformed to some more personal zone.
Not even tasting soon, nor caring for prickers,
we feel ripeness alone, we blackberry pickers.

Firefly

As a child, I was told that I was a star,
whose brilliance would light up the world like a jar
filled with fireflies. In that place I grew up,
we'd crouch in dark grass, catching them in the cup
of a hand that quickly transformed into heart,
a roseate, luminescent, star part.
From our palms, we poured them into a glass,
so that we could catch more, faster than fast.
Then, everything changed. Maybe it was the time
when the man I had loved would no longer be mine,
or when all the freedom I'd anticipated
could no longer be fully emancipated.
Jobs couldn't be quit, hours must be put in,
the soiled re-washed, the fanciful shut in.
My erstwhile fresh talent soon felt like old rot;
I had to be happy with what I had got.
Now, when I think back to that life as a star,
I see less of the firefly, more of the jar:
the air holes on top we made with a pick
used to pry nuts from shells, a sharp metal stick.
It tore holes that were cutting, jagged beneath,
and could easily pierce an insect's bright sheath.
I think of those holes, the sharp underside
that ceilinged that glow, that unreasoning pride.

Porch

The porch pulled them to its side,
invited nestling upon shaded planks,
recalled cool soft times, clover in fields,
the day she cut his hair, and then they picked
out smooth flat stones,
lining them along its surface, thick with
years of knobby deck paint. Against it,
the stones shone like perfect moons to plant upon
winter tabletops, reminders
that nights sown by fireflies
were going on somewhere, some time.

Pink

Trees full of blossom, the night smells pink
though it's black, a thick summer darkness
barely held back by window screen.
I hear dishes in the sink, a familiar clatter,
and think of the summer kitchen
of my youth (my grandma's), where the women wiped

the dishes, too many for the rack, wiped
the oilclothed table too; the men, skin pink
from glossy food, escaped the kitchen
glare, slinking into the darkness
of the den, the chatty TV clatter
a sound fluorescence against the dim screen.

There too, we were protected by a screen
from bites, buzz, wing, and the wind that wiped
that stretched-flat land, a soft clatter
of night and grass and damp that blew towards the pink
edge of dawn, an engine of chill darkness
that was only truly blocked by the glow of kitchen

yellow. I watched one aunt in the kitchen,
amazed that she never even tried to screen
her keen sense of life's darkness.
When she looked at my grandmother, she often wiped
her eyes, and sniffing, face too pink,
cleaned with a banging clatter.

Though she was always a center of clatter,
that aunt. She had a kind of two-walled kitchen
in her own house, open; and wore hot pink,
played jokes, charades, a half-hearted screen
of despondency, still, the good housewife, she wiped
the smallest speck from her counters. Her own darkness

seeming inevitable, it was a darkness
she hurried towards, smoking, drinking hard, the clatter
of uncertainty (as to timing) wiped
her out. In the meantime, she cleaned—my grandma's kitchen
after her death, and, at the Funeral Home, made a quick screen
of the corpse. "That lipstick's way too pink,"

she hissed, then wiped my grandma's lips like a kitchen
stain. Despite the clatter in my brain, I served as screen,
a guard in the blossomed darkness, as she rubbed off pink.

Wondrous

We flew out there, then drove.
My mother, who despised gum chewers,
snapped hers loudly, pushing herself up
to the wheel as if it were the chin rest
at an eye exam.

Though my grandmother lived in Minnesota, the hospital
was in Iowa. When the rental car crossed state lines—
another source of amazement—
my mother, who only drove set routes, had rented a car—
the road narrowed and curved and my mother
cursed all Republicans.
She took the thin gravelly shoulder as
a personal affront; the lip the tires
skidded against was even worse,
an insult to FDR.

At the hospital, my grandmother's hair cast
about her face like a bridal veil blown back.
She was better already, she said, just
at the sight of us *(but we sure shouldn't have come;
it was too darn hard.)*
Then pointed to a cup of jello,
which was as crimson, faceted, as a ruby,
and, at first, resisted my spoon.
"*Mama,*" my mother said.

Dressed

The sweater swallows.
As the mother pulls at the fabric, the child,
between whines,
gulps the dark warm air inside the warp.
At last, the head burps into a room that tastes
like sky after that tightness.
The mother does not think back to the child's birth,
but only sips the relief of something that
has to be done, being done.

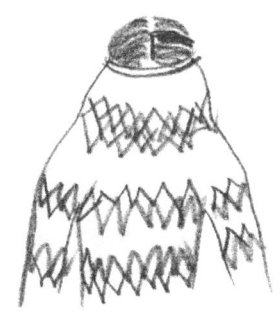

Going in to look at my daughter asleep

When I walk into your room
I try to sneak
beneath your soft
small breaths like
hiding inside the
lilac bush, trying not to laugh, like
the dreams in which I
sit with my dead
grandmother, so happy to
have her back. It's a rebirth
each time I see you after
not seeing you; it's
as if you miracle made
the dead rise.

No chance

I wanted to give her time, a summer's day,
a perfect green blue day that I would pluck
from my summers to come, that I would lay
upon her bed, and, shimmering, tuck
around her. It should have been an easy offer,
easy to say. After all, the future
can't be readily assigned; life's coffer
holds nothing forfeit. Tubes followed suture
to a darkness barely gowned; I searched around
my jangling brain for words, but what came out
were stones that lined her pillow, the sound
not meaning my meaning, and not about
summer days; my own fierce will to live
hoarding what I had no power to give.

Home

Her cheekbones, Cherokee, she'd told me
when we were younger, have
reasserted themselves. Last visit
her face was swollen, foreshortened by
pink scarf, but hair has grown
what with the end of the chemo
into small feathery clumps,
and her features, that web of
intent-filled bone, have resurfaced.
You look so beautiful, I say. Smile
flickers until she turns again to
trying to sit up, though we have
to catch and lift and
her husband
to support her,
which she cannot
bear for long. But
I have to get up, she says,
I have to get out of this place.

He talks of brushing her hair first,
fingering brief curls. This
brings a nod. She has been naturally
beautiful her whole life,
but also a beauty who brushed hair first.
But I've got to get home, she insists
suddenly, arching away.
You are home, he tells her, in

your own room, your own bed,
but she pushes now so hard
that we have to turn
her legs, gather her arms, lift and walk
her to a chair, its chintz print
roses on vines, then, when she can't sit,
walk her back.

Did you call the car? Tell him
to come right now? You've got
to call it.
I called it, her husband lies
as he holds her head close to slide down drops.
But I've got to go home, she cries, pulling away
from body, pain, still air.
Just stay for a bit, he whispers.

The Last Thing
For Rhona Saffer

Know that,
when I must go,
I will love you
just the same.

When I must go,
I know it will not feel
just the same.
There will be cool air—

I know it will not feel
like my lips—
but there will be cool air
caressing your face

like my lips,
while your smile only,
caressing your face
(oh reflection of mine),

will be your smile only.
I never wanted to cause you pain,
oh reflection of mine.
That was the last thing

I ever wanted to cause you. Pain.
No, I would love you—
that was the last thing.
Just the same,

know I would love you,
I will love you,
just the same.
Know that.

What Funerals Are For

I worried that I might not be able to stop
the posturing that shaped my busy mind—
all I'd see, all whom I might know,
imagined encounters over funeral supper wine.

The posturing, the shape of busy mind,
dwarfed the Jesus-coated windows, babes in stone
(imagined encounters over Last Supper wine),
when fingers touching lid, they led it down.

Dwarfing the Jesus-coated windows, babes in stone,
a block of wood, of over-polished grain,
as fingers touching lid, they led it down,
pulling with it, a winding sheet of heaving pain.

A block of wood, of over-polished grain—
I knew she couldn't breathe there, that she'd no more breath
pulling within a winding sheet of heaving pain,
weeping without will, without relief.

I knew she couldn't breathe there, that she'd no more breath,
and all I saw, all whom I might know,
weeping without will, without relief.
I worried that I might not be able to stop.

Burned Soldier (A Mask For Face)

He tried to smile but found that skin would balk;
a mask for face was not what he had planned.
Right action should give rise to right result,

saving the day as it called on God to halt
all burn and bite of bomb as if by wand;
he tried to smile but found that skin would balk.

When they talked of graft, he always thought of molt,
as if his flesh held feathers that could span
right action, then give rise to right result—

cheeks that were smooth but rough, but loose but taut—
it all had been so easy as a man.
He tried to smile but found that skin would balk.

Hate helped at times; to think it was their fault.
But how could "they" be numbered? Like grains of sand,
like actions that give rise to like result,

like eyes that fit in lids not white as salt—
this lead white face was not what he had planned.
He tried to smile but found that skin would balk;
right action should give rise to right result.

Shattering

The shattering of lives should take some time.
It shouldn't come in flashes, clods of dirt,
no moment for altered course, for change of mind.

The actual choice ahead should be well-signed,
the frailty of good luck, a blood-soaked shirt;
the shattering of lives should take some time.

He knew that road was risky, heard a whine,
but in the end those warnings were too curt,
no moment for altered course, for change of mind.

Hard to foresee your own true body lined
with metal plates and plastic tubes of hurt;
the shattering of lives should take some time.

So many hours after to refine
what happened in that second's blinding lurch,
no moment for altered course or change of mind.

Or was it fate? A studied path, not whim?
His heart tried hard to measure out the worth
of shattering lives. It would take some time,
without moment for altering course or mind.

In the Ukraine, Sixty-some Years Later, Still Finding
For the Reverend Patrick Desbois, documenting the Holocaust

Reluctant shovels prod earth;
roots grip hard; growth
took well here, the ground
not trod by paths, boots,
only (maybe) light feet running on a dare,
and the dart of swallows, a swivel of darkness
against blue-violet, evening sky.
The underdirt unfolds in webs
of stem as pale as bone,
as fine as hair that might have grown pale too.
Men pause, leaning against
shovels' grosgrain necks; it feels
like gasoline coming up,
a poison that must come out, that wants to come out,
still burns. "This was the place?"
The priest's voice reminds them of rock—worn, smooth,
soft, hard, a color that seems to them indeterminate
(at least, they don't know what it's called).
Looking down from beneath wool caps,
they swallow, looser collars limp against scrubbed
necks, then dig again.

Too late to bargain.
Yellowed pages have been
produced; the prints of names —
the smudged "A" of

"AVRAHAM," the terminal H of
"DEVORAH"—have been again
recorded. Dark eyes' insistence
on having once seen, has been seen.
Burns coming up, those digging
want to spit it out
but can't, not here.

Honor Killing

The knife slides in,
with force.
She is thinner than he has remembered,
her collarbone sharp as
a hook he thrashes against.
Mind snags on heart, but
cannot aim for breast,
only the knife can look past nipple.
Smaller than he's remembered,
with too-soft skin that folds within
whites of eyes as big as blade.
He tries to think
of flame, but blood
fountains,
in honor of
the righteous,
fountains.
Why has she made him,
righteous,
do this,
with force?

Heard on the Esplanade, a Pantoum

The woman cries
that she doesn't believe it.
Don't tell me lies.
She pulls away from him.

That she doesn't believe it—
Is that what you're telling me?
She pulls away from him
in the sun of the walkway.

Is that what you're telling me?
Sky overbright on sleeves
in the sun of the walkway
twists the fall of fall leaves.

Sky overbright on sleeves
he holds onto. Her, she tries to tear,
twists, the fall of fall leaves.
All pretend not to hear.

He holds onto her. She tries to tear.
Tried to rape me, rings out.
All pretend not to hear.
How can she, how can she not—

Tried to rape me, rings out.
Don't tell me lies.
How can she, how can she not?
The woman cries.

Courbet

All I can say is that
it's a good thing we have museums
hanging Courbets,
Rubens,
Rembrandts,
the occasional Italian,
with their depictions of swelling bellies,
dimples gathered around spines, flesh rippling
like Aphrodite's birth foam,
the creep of pubic hair juxtaposed by coy hands
whose curved digits
pudge, slightly sunken cheeks (above, below),
spidery blood vessels
rooting beneath the patina.
All I can say, as I catch
my face in the glass,
glance down at my folio
of torso, is that
it's a good thing.

Kali

Dear Kali, you are my favorite goddess.
It is your krazy hair,
and all those men that you wear
at your waist.
It is the way that you waste
them in your big mouth;
that you break them in two with your teeth.

Dear Kali, you are my favorite goddess.
It is the way that you slit,
the way that you split,
the way that you pit
them against each other, heads against heads,
and that sharp spear that you hold
in your hand.

Dear Kali, you are my favorite goddess.
Make me your third eye.
Make me the clasp at your waist.
Give me the weight of fifty men, the hook of the chain.
Dear Kali, you are my favorite.

Thin Birthday

On one birthday when she was very thin,
he brought out, after much whispering,
a half grapefruit set upon a platter.

It was their birthday cake platter—wooden,
painted with blue ribbon swirl, holes put in
careful spaces along its perimeter.

The lone half grapefruit balanced in the place
for cake; a pink candle centering its face
like a faded, twisted cherry, stretched out tall.

He looked at her with such worry, not
(she thought) for her condition, but to please. What
to give a child stuck in rigid refusal?

She'd disdain cake, she'd groan (he knew), *oh Dad*.
So, for her to weep, to get so very sad,
was quite unfair. *I wanted to give you*

something you would take, he said, as they sat
out in the car and he awkwardly pat
her arm, reaching for something flesh and true.

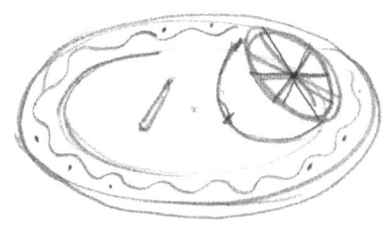

Daughter Needing to Practice the Tango

She wants me to do what I can't.
Luckily, she also wants to be better than me.
So, after the initial frustration,
it works out just fine.

In the Stairwell

Descending the building's stairs, she feels her breast,
fumbling beneath her bra to get to skin,
palpating (as they say) but in a mess
of here and there and not all within
the confines of an organized exam.
Silly to do it here, not time or place,
someone else might come, have to move her hand,
and yet fear seems to justify the race,
as if by checking each time it crosses mind,
especially checking fast, she can avoid
ever finding anything of the kind
that should not be found. And so, devoid
of caution, but full of care nonetheless,
she steps slowly down the stairs, feeling her breast.

A Woman Needing to Pee

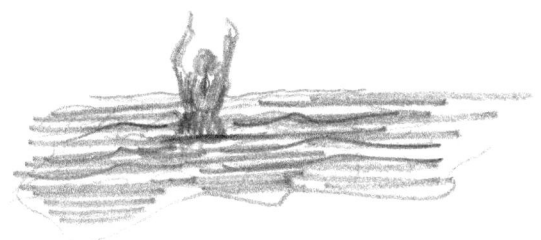

A woman needing to pee,
she steps into the sea, knees
salt, a piercing balm, her
shaved legs grimace, gasp
cold, still she strolls thighward,
as far as she is able, needing to pee,
squats needing to hide it,
rubs water over her arms to hide it better,
acting out a woman too timid
to go out far, a woman
needing to cool herself. But
she craves warmth and secretes it,
secret warmth, wet-warming
all the sea.
Stretching tall,
and cold now only where air
licks skin, she dives
into the afterglow,
a woman who swims.

Mismatched Couple

She skidded along the surface of time.
He dug his heels in, feet flexed.
Either way time flowed,
bunching around his ankles,
throwing up spray with her each sharp swerve.

They tried to hold hands,
but it was difficult.
Even side by side was
a stretch, and when he dug in,
wake deepening, and she lurched, angling away,
great elasticity was needed.

Travelers' Wedding – Bangkok

The monsoon sky grew slowly thick with grey
as sweat like traffic stalled the steaming city.
It didn't feel much like the first of May,

not even in his shirt saved for the day,
nor in the Indian skirt she'd thought so pretty.
The monsoon sky grew slowly thick with grey

as they hurried to the bureau where they'd say
"I do," or if required, some learned Thai ditty.
It didn't feel much like the first of May;

still was, and, as they found, a holiday.
Closed office doors made clean clothes somehow gritty;
the monsoon sky grew slowly thick with grey.

"Tomorrow then," they sighed, feigning dismay,
and making jokes that almost passed for witty.
But it didn't feel much like the first of May,

stained, like his shirt, with portent and delay
as sweat, like lifetimes, stalled throughout the city.
The monsoon sky grew slowly thick with grey;
it didn't feel much like the first of May.

Cowspotting

He said that cows always faced
in the same direction.
As in Mecca? she asked, sarcastic.
As in a field, he corrected.
You just look in any field, he said.
*The cows will all be facing
the same way.*

They curved around a
country road, which passed shallow hills spotted
with the honey brown shanks of still cattle.
Look, she said, *that one's
completely sideways.*
An anomaly, he said. *The exception
that proves the rule. There's always one.*

If he was someone who had to be right, she
was someone who had to be righter.

For years afterwards,
even though she got to the country only occasionally,
she carefully checked the collective stance
of cows, never accepting a near unanimity of
moist soft snout.

For No Good Reason

For no good reason, my body begins
to ooze, the moisture creeping
out between my legs like a stealthy animal
furry but small as a bug
that loves to cuddle.
Imagined hair on end, delicate
as the eyelash of a cat, it traces
its movements upon my thighs,
then circles to find rest.
We go to sleep together.

Second Marriage

He's the kind of guy who carefully seasons
an iron skillet, oiling the surface,
eschewing soap. I know all the reasons,
understand rust, stickiness; nonetheless,
I squeeze Dawn right onto the blackness,
and, when I smell that low-heated oil, I
rebel. "*Are you,*" I charge (nearly senseless),
"*seasoning my frying pan?*" As if to try
traditional method, some slow process
of caretaking, were a sure scheme to defy,
deny, descry, the rushed independence
I've professed, those hurry-up lone years I
scraped so many sharp implements across,
getting rid of the hard bits, loss and loss.

Lovers

A badinage of mist parleyed
the dawn outside their window,
a silken warp of grey like, but not
like, the jism that
glistened upon her belly. He rubbed
it carefully upward,
telling her how good it was
for her skin. For her part,
she wondered at the swiftness with which
the desire to keep him inside had given way
to relief that he hadn't been. Then they turned,
as not-quite-paired as two breeze-blown leaves, the silver
glint of their underveins upended.

Mist

Mist rises over lake like
firs sighing like
awe inspiring like
hope dying (not needed, not even considered), like
dawn breaking like
love making like
water curling in its fall,
like head on lap on
lips on lips
on you on me,
like fingers fingering
(brushing against a nipple
or being brushed against),
like something somewhere sure
of joy,
like the thing itself.

Yoga Haiku

Mula Bandha—genital
smile. I'd walk a mile
to be in your yoga class.

Truest Love

The little dog lay on its back
in the semblance of
truest love.
The woman, leaning in from above, ignored
stained whiskers and breath like fish,
in the semblance of truest love.

The little dog exalted when she came home
as if she were its dearest wish,
the answer to heart's prayer.
She said, 'hey there,' and stooped
to capture some wriggle.

The little dog saw her as
itself spelled backwards; she
accepted the role, thankful that
some being had finally taken
due note of her
existence, ignoring
breath like fish.

Side

All day I've seen your side
in my mind, the smooth slopes
of joint and limb like
the banks of a river.
All day I've strained towards these banks
with an overflow of self,
that wash of discontent,
too quick, too fretful, to find anything
but what's next and next and next.
All day I've longed to stretch out by some cove
in your warm torso—
you're so sound in sleep—
to slide between bone, flesh,
to subside.

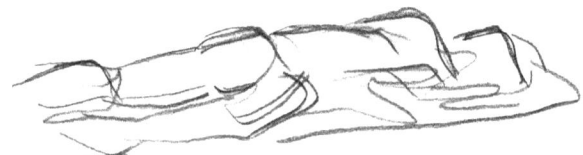

After the Fights

If you were sleeping beside me now, I'd
ease myself to your cock, hoping
to catch you dreaming (but not
about commandoes, bears, fights—
anything at all that warranted repulse.)
I'd take you,
already hard from inner flight,
into my mouth until a woman sidestroked through
your REM, then
maneuver myself up
your belly directing the thrust
from throat to cunt—you'd probably
have woken now, the sheets of the subconscious
thrown off.
I'd press my hands against
the small of your back as if you might try to escape—
you wouldn't—
and all the times I've ever threatened the end
of this, you/me, would be
but a dream, never having
happened in this world. I would know,
from my side of the fuck, my luck at having a man
who'd find in this moment
the absolute truth.

Facts

With careful trunks, elephants sift dry bones.
Some humans wonder if it means anything.
I'm not one of them. I hear intent groans,
specific moans, directed stomping;
imagine lined eyes embedding tears,
memories of dust baths in the savannah.
I probably go overboard; my gears
are set to the emotive; the manna
from my heaven is to be served to all.
I see what I look for, sure. Still, when I
step back, look at facts, even what others call
facts, there is that which makes the heart cry:
the trunks of elephants stippled with care,
caressing the bones of fellows not there.

9/11

The burning buildings woke me from a sleep
of what I thought important, nothing now.
I ran hard down the smoking, crumbling street,

praying that my child was mine to keep,
dear God oh please dear God I whispered loud;
the burning buildings woke me from a sleep.

Some stopped to stare, all of us to weep
as eyes replayed the towers' brutal bow.
I ran hard down the smoking, crumbling street,

north sky a startling blue, the south a heap
of man-wrought cloud; I pushed against the crowd;
the burning buildings woke me from a sleep.

I'd never complain again, never treat
with trivial despair—or so I vowed.
I ran hard down the smoking, crumbling street.

I'd change, give thanks—I saw them leap—
and begged for all the grace God would allow.
The burning buildings woke me from a sleep;
I ran hard down the smoking, crumbling street.

Snippets

I wake with snippets of prayer in my head,
the Lord's Prayer, only one I really know,
which, mixed with plainer appeals, makes my bed
a swirl of hallowed and dear God. I sow
the phrases with care, though half asleep,
the mother guarding her young by any means.
Unsure of God, I ask Him still to keep
my children close, then, in case this God leans
towards the literal, add "not too close."
I circle the prayer, moving in, out,
sidestepping chemistry, that ionic host,
religious precept too. What this is about
is fear, the omnipresent threat of grief
a power beyond all disbelief.

Post-Eden

Before the sky, a lovely pale, a boy,
tall on glistening grass, tosses a ball,
and I wonder why it is that joy
is not simply inhaled. Is it the Fall
that keeps us from feeling how it lines
the air we breathe? Is it that first loss
that keeps us toiling within the confines
of our skins, unheeding unhidden cost?
A soft haze, like a blessing, nestles on
the sea, mutes the horizon, brings the far near.
So much within reach. The brain wrestles on
in its hardscrabble way, yet slowly fear
unwinds, diminished by sky, sea, view.
An inner hand makes the catch, more too.

No Nest

These words are no nest. They won't warm you
when I'm gone. You won't be able to tuck
your head under a *t*, though it starts true,
slip fingers down *n*'s curve, deftly pluck
replies from even the unsilent *e*'s.
They won't warm me either—no echoes
in ashen brains, even spread upon a breeze.
As twigs and hair and grass and lint close in,
words will be somewhere else, just as what peeps
behind these eyes, this voice, this flickering
insistent maw of self, will, at best, sleep
long. But for now, I'm here, a bickering
steadfast wordmonger, building a place
of syllabic lingering, would-be embrace.

No Matter

Yesterday in the dim fluorescence
of subway car, I thought of molecules.
They seemed, in that greyed light, the essence
of life. I saw them stretched in pools,
sometimes seemingly limpid, other times
volcanic, fervidly swooping me
abubble, then mucking me into slimes
of laval woe, a test tube of to be
or not to be. Today, I'm by the sea,
and water, vaster than pools, sparkles
under light so immense it cannot be
broken down for parts, yet its particles
raise up the non-molecular part
of me, what refuses to lose heart,
no matter—

Villanelle to Wandering Brain

Sometimes my mind feels like it's lost its way
and must make do with words that are in reach
as pink as dusk (not dawn), the half-light of the day,

when what it craves is crimson, noon in May,
the unscathed verb or complex forms of speech.
But sometimes my mind feels like it's lost its way

and calls the egg a lightbulb, plan a tray,
and no matter how it search or how beseech
is pink as dusk (not dawn), the half-light of the day.

I try to make a joke of my decay
or say that busy-ness acts as the leech
that makes my mind feel like it's lost its way,

but whole years seem as spent as last month's pay,
plundered in unmet dares to eat a peach—
as pink as dusk (not dawn), the half-light of the day.

There is so much I think I still should say,
so press poor words like linens to heart's breach,
but find my mind has somehow lost its way
as pink as dusk (not dawn), the half-light of the day.

Colaba Night (Mumbai)

Rows of people lie swaddled, exhausted ghosts,
even their pale cloth coverings wilted,
rolling up at the edges like a hard life's feet.
Why do they line up so far from the sidewalk, out
on the street?
Rats the major activity,
cats looking frightened.

After it's fallen

In Benares, the tenders rake the fallen feet back into the flames.
The first time we watched them, I was horrified.
How you would know that foot, I kept thinking,
your father's soft purply big-veined foot.
My father's feet have always seemed too small to me.
When he walks he seems to go on edge, as if they
can hardly carry him.
The toes of his shoes turn up strangely,
even after he's had them just one week,
Something from the war, he's always said.

In Benares, the feet are the last parts to be burned.
They overhang the pyre and simply
wait there, smoking slowly
until the shins are completely charred.
Their full flesh too heavy for the burned legs,
they fall, eventually, to the ground.
They never fall together, but one first, pointing randomly,
the other still flexed in the air.

When one of the tenders notices, he
pushes the fallen foot back into the flames.
He uses two long poles, the

green bamboos of the bier.
Sometimes he has to lever the foot
to reach the flames again, crossing the poles
like huge chopsticks.

They have dark feet in Benares,
darker than my father's would be,
smooth and brown.
I couldn't stop looking at them, thinking how you would know
that foot on the ground there, that foot.

East Indian Trains in the Catskills
For Jeannie Hutchins

As lilacs cast their fragrance on wet grass,
she thinks of trains and dust, the smell of hot spiced chai,
maroon banquettes, babbled cries en masse—
muffled by shutters echoed Hindi words for buy,
the soles of porters' shoes so flat and white and pointed,
her own were thick, protection sewn by Clarks,
the baseline of what made her feel anointed—
when her hand waved at the window, it left sparks.
She sparkled just for coming from the West
(with cash, pale eyes, and shockingly blonde hair).
But now she feels a different specialness:
no matter where she is, she once was there,
so that even on this Catskill-scented lawn,
mind resonates with Indian trains at dawn.

Jaipur

Cold inside, I foolishly drink
two cups of strong hot tea.
Now I will sit awake all night
thinking of you.

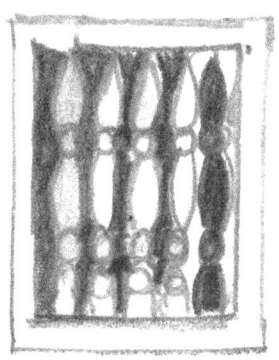

ACKNOWLEDGEMENTS

My deepest thanks to those whose specific help, encouragement and love has meant more to me than I can ever express (even in a villanelle): my very dear Jason Martin, Meredith Martin, Christina Martin, Diana Barco, and Jeannie Hutchins.

Additional thanks to Sigma Andrea Torres and Diana Barco for their endless patience with my endless revisions.

Thanks, too, to all my old writing buddies: Susan Ramsay, Rosemary Carroll, Katie Goldberg, Caroline Brickman, Paul P. Gustafson, and again, Christina, Meredith, Jay, Jeannie and Diana. Special thanks to the readers of my ManicDDaily blog whose interest has been wonderfully encouraging and inspiring.

And, finally, thanks to my beloved parents, Paul and Phyllis Gustafson, and my very tolerant boss, Rob Muffly.

K.P.E.G.

BackStroke Books

Karin Gustafson and Diana Barco have been friends since their previous lifetimes.

Karin lives in New York City and divides her time between practicing law and practicing writing. She also practices the art of illustration, primarily with elephants, as may be seen in her children's book *1 Mississippi*, and her ManicDDaily blog.

Diana lives in Bogota, Colombia. An architect and artist, she has been dedicated to sexual and reproductive health and rights through her work with IPPF for many years. She is also founding member of the Rogelio Salmona Foundation.

www.ingramcontent.com/pod-product-compliance
Lightning Source LLC
Chambersburg PA
CBHW031417040426
42444CB00005B/611